I0468997

PERIHACKS | P.O. Box 2713 | Austin, TX 78768-2713
http://perihacks.com

"Finding That Needle in the Haystack Periscope Client in 5 Days (10 Easy Steps)"

Copyright 2016 © reserved by Arvin Poole

Website: http://www.PeriHacks.com
Email: arvin@perihacks.com

Bulk Ordering Information:
Special discounts are available on quantity purchases by corporations, associations, and others. For details, contact the publisher at the email address above.

Orders by U.S. trade bookstores and wholesalers contact the offices of www.PeriHacks.com at the contact information above.

Social Media Platforms: @ArvinPoole
Printed in the United States of America

ISBN-13:
978-1530999606

ISBN-10:
153099960X

PERIHACKS | P.O. Box 2713 | Austin, TX 78768-2713
http://perihacks.com

FINDING THAT NEEDLE IN THE

HAYSTACK

PERISCOPE.TV CLIENT IN 5 DAYS

(10 EASY STEPS)

ARVIN POOLE

PERIHACKS | P.O. Box 2713 | Austin, TX 78768-2713
http://perihacks.com

PERIHACKS | P.O. Box 2713 | Austin, TX 78768-2713
http://perihacks.com

TABLE OF CONTENTS

PERIHACKS | P.O. Box 2713 | Austin, TX 78768-2713
http://perihacks.com

PERIHACKS | P.O. Box 2713 | Austin, TX 78768-2713
http://perihacks.com

10 Easy Steps: To Find the Needle in the Haystack

Eager to secure your first client on Periscope? In this book you will find (10) ten teachable steps that I've taken to make my first sale on the fastest growing live streaming application.

Before we think twice about pressing that Red Button to start a Periscope.tv broadcast, to push our products and services; there are some strict, unwritten and unspoken rules of doing business on Periscope:

First, you must have the mindset that success on Periscope.tv is not about vanity numbers, i.e. number of followers, number of hearts or number of broadcast shares. It all boils down to your bottom line and converting leads to sales.

Second, your business doesn't end with a sale. It begins with a sale. Going through each of the (10) ten steps outlined in this book is only a guide to get you to the beginning. It is what you must go through to start your journey in live-streaming.

And last, your Periscope.tv profile and bio must be polished and up to date. I've written these with the reader in mind and I believe that anyone can flourish on this application with the following in mind.

PERIHACKS | P.O. Box 2713 | Austin, TX 78768-2713
http://perihacks.com

Smile! I See Your Profile Photo

Quite different in other social media platforms that target businesses, your profile photo should not be your business logo. It should be a professional headshot that exemplifies the brand that you want your potential prospects to see you (the owner) and your company as. When it comes to your personal brand, it's important that your image extends from your profile to your live broadcasts.

The Periscope.tv Bio

Only 150 characters? Say, what?! Yes, I know. However, this is the perfect location for your company's tagline or value proposition. Even though this space holds the maximum of 150 characters, like Twitter, I strongly suggest that you keep it short, relevant and not afraid to be creative. Who wants to read a boring job description? Let's add your personality into it. Bottom line, it is your personality and character that your clients find relatable and trusting.

Here are a couple of examples of creative, yet relatable, Periscope.tv Profile Bio's:

Profile: @AzaniaNoah

Bio: Award-winning singer/songwriter | Vocal Coach ❦ #TheVoice ❦ Joy & Inspiration! ❦ Join

Fans: 👫 http://bit.ly/teamazania ❦

ALBUM: 🤍 http://Azania.com/album/rising

PERIHACKS | P.O. Box 2713 | Austin, TX 78768-2713
http://perihacks.com

Profile: @MrRelentless

Bio: International Motivational Speaker, Personal Development Coach & Author. Motivation & Inspiration Daily!  BAM! http://Facebook.com/MrRelentless10X

Website | Blog | Landing Page |

Social Media Platforms

Another important part of your Periscope.tv bio is to add a web URL link that connects to a site or page that provides more information about you, the products that you are selling, and/or an event that you are promoting. In the marketing world, we refer to this page as a landing page. If you do not have a page or site to link to, your social media profile page, i.e. Twitter, Facebook or Instagram, would be perfect places to send your Periscope.tv viewers to. Just ensure that the social media profile that you refer your viewers to align with the content of your Periscope.tv bio.

Now that you understand some of the unwritten and unspoken rules of doing business on Periscope.tv, it's now time to begin your journey of securing your first customer leveraging the Periscope.tv app!

STEP ONE

Develop a Five Part Scope Series

Let's first ask ourselves "What business am I in? What products or services do I provide? What is the makeup of my ideal customer?" Now think about what are the challenges that your ideal customer faces and how will your product or service help them. This may sound like a daunting task, but you can learn a lot about your targeted customer just by paying attention to the comments when you are live broadcasting. But in order to get your viewers to talk about their challenges, your content must connect with them on a personal and human level. You are not focusing on your product or service features. You are focusing on the benefits that your product or service provides that tackles a pain point!

Next step is to come up with your list of five customer pain points and five corresponding benefits of your product or service. Each pain point and corresponding benefit will be your topic for each day of the week.

General rules of thumb

Focus on delivering targeted content that: a) addresses a pain point b) adds value to your audience and c) educates your audience.

STEP TWO

Five Consecutive Days

Scope each day for five consecutive days with the intention of GIVING, GIVING, GIVING! Your goal is to provide value-added content with ZERO expectation of return. Remember that consistency is KEY! When purchasing items online or during a live broadcast, people are more likely to buy from those who they know. It's like a relationship. The more you get to know a person, the more likely you are to enter into a committed relationship with them.

PERIHACKS | P.O. Box 2713 | Austin, TX 78768-2713
http://perihacks.com

PERIHACKS | P.O. Box 2713 | Austin, TX 78768-2713
http://perihacks.com

STEP THREE

Probe Viewers Challenges

After your scope introduction, this is the perfect opportunity to start off your content with the following question: *"What are your biggest challenges in your business?"*

This may seem redundant after Days 2 and 3, but keep in mind that you will be attracting new viewers to your scopes each time that you live broadcast. It is important to be consistent throughout this step.

PERIHACKS | P.O. Box 2713 | Austin, TX 78768-2713
http://perihacks.com

PERIHACKS | P.O. Box 2713 | Austin, TX 78768-2713
http://perihacks.com

STEP FOUR

Daily Focus Key

As stated in STEP ONE, each day you will focus on ONE key Challenge and associated Benefit or Solution(s) to that Challenge. Below is an example that will help you with your content:

(A) *WHAT are the Challenges that Your Viewers' Face?* These are the stated challenges that your viewers have expressed.

(B) *WHY do they face these Challenges?* Now you must step outside of your viewers' individual challenges and address the potential causes or inputs to them.

PERIHACKS | P.O. Box 2713 | Austin, TX 78768-2713
http://perihacks.com

(C) *What is the benefit that addresses each Challenge?* This is your stated solution(s) to your viewers' challenges.

NOTE: Day (1) One, you will need to have your challenge topic already defined. After Day 1, you are now prepared to gather feedback from your viewers to develop topics for Days 2-5. If you lack gathering feedback from your viewers, directly solicit feedback from your friends through your other social media channels, i.e. Facebook, Twitter, etc. It will be important to have your remaining challenge topics before moving forward to STEP 5.

STEP FIVE

Segmentation Power

For each viewer that provides their challenges, segment them in a list so that you have a better understanding of your viewers' needs.

Your segmented list needs to have a theme that is focused on the pain point(s) of your customer. You will begin your Scope Series on Monday and it will end on Friday. The reason that we start on Monday and not on any other day is because we want a back-to-back series during the week and not to linger into the weekend. We would like to capture an audience during working days.

PERIHACKS | P.O. Box 2713 | Austin, TX 78768-2713
http://perihacks.com

Now, let's look at an example of segmentation power, which I have used:

Let's say that you are in the fitness business which is a very broad topic. But let's say that you are in the business of helping a customer build up their physique for an upcoming competition, hence fitness competition. One of the pain points could be a lack of motivation. Your customer is having a difficult time staying motivated to move forward in preparation for competing. So, the Segmentation Theme that addresses this pain point could be *"How Do Go from Zero to Hero for Your Next Fitness Competition"*. Then you break up each day *(Monday, Tuesday,*

Wednesday, Thursday and Friday) with one specific pain point per day. Each pain point will be addressed with at least one benefit or solution.

Your pain point for each day could look like this:

- ***(Monday)*** Pain Point: *"I lose track of when I need to work-out due to my work schedule!"*

  Solution: Make a schedule, and stick to it!

- ***(Tuesday)*** Pain Point: *"I get de-motivated when working alone"*

  Solution: Find a community!

- ***(Wednesday)*** Pain Point: *"I have a tough time figuring out which exercise routines are working!"*

Solution: Keep a workout log!

- **(Thursday)** Pain Point: *"After several weeks of the same routine, I lose interest!"*

  Solution: Create goals!

- **(Friday)** Pain Point: *"After a week of sticking to my workout schedule, I am exhausted and mentally drained!"*

  Solution: Take a break and give yourself a reward!

Rule of Thumb

Each daily point should result in a Scope with one-tip. Keep your scopes within 30 minutes and address one specific bullet point item per day and provide one solution per pain point.

PERIHACKS | P.O. Box 2713 | Austin, TX 78768-2713
http://perihacks.com

STEPS SIX & SEVEN

Cultivate, Nurture and Repeat / Viewer Qualification

<u>Cultivate, Nurture and Repeat</u>: It is important to nurture this process by repeating this process through each of the 5 scopes.

NOTE: You should NEVER contact anyone at this time without their permission. That is SPAM and is a bad thing to do in Marketing.

<u>Viewer Qualification</u>: After the 1st four scopes of providing VALUE-ADDED content and polling your viewers, you should now have qualified those who are serious about needing your help.

PERIHACKS | P.O. Box 2713 | Austin, TX 78768-2713
http://perihacks.com

STEP EIGHT

The Scope Reward Offer

On the 5th Scope (Day 5), extend an offer for a Complimentary one-on-one Discovery Session to all viewers that attended your LIVE Scope.

This will be done through the following steps:

a) **Setup an Email System** (MailChimp, Mailer Lite, AWeber, Get Response, etc.) so that you can now begin to capture emails.

b) **Set-up a Landing Page** that provides a brief introduction of (1) who you are (2) what you provide (3) how you can help with your services and (4) A Call-To-Action, i.e. Sign-up for 1:1 Discovery Session, Download Free Report, etc. If you are have a WordPress site and seeking a landing page solution, I highly recommend the popular plugin, Thrive Landing Pages.

c) **Secure a Memorable Link** from bit.ly, goo.gl or other URL shortened services. If you have a WordPress website, I also recommend using a plugin such as Pretty Links which allows you to use your own branded domain to as a URL shortener. It also tracks each hit on your URL and provides a full, detailed report of where the hit came from, the browser, operating system and host.

d) **BONUS OFFER,** such as a Free PDF Download or Report. Examples could be a brief summary of what you would cover in your 1:1, a summary of one of your related scopes or an Industry Report of the market that you serve.

E) **Share your Link** at the end of each scope!

PERIHACKS | P.O. Box 2713 | Austin, TX 78768-2713
http://perihacks.com

STEPS NINE & TEN

Warm Lead(s) Validation / Follow Through
& Fulfill the Request

Warm Lead Validation: Pay attention to those
who sign up to your email list. Is there anyone in
your list that you previously segmented? If so,
then you have qualified and validated a lead and
moved them into the WARM lead bucket.

Follow Through & Fulfill the Request: You are
now at the end and where many of us freeze up.
Steps 1 - 9 prepare you to ASK FOR THE SALE!
You have qualified your leads and now it is time
to fulfill the request with your warm leads within

PERIHACKS | P.O. Box 2713 | Austin, TX 78768-2713
http://perihacks.com

24 hours to secure a Date/Time for a Complimentary one-on-one Session!

PERIHACKS | P.O. Box 2713 | Austin, TX 78768-2713
http://perihacks.com

THE BONUS PRIZE

Low Risk, High Reward

The reward for making it through each of the (10) ten steps is rewarded when you receive an email for a quote for services or a PayPal notification that your digital product was purchased. I am not sure about you, but that is an exhilarating feeling to receive money in my account. It validates everything that I worked hard for.

Unfortunately, many business owners miss out on getting this far in the process because they don't understand that each step is the next step to the sale, which is the start and not the end. We give up too quickly before we are able to see the results of the work that we put in. We claim defeat without truly understanding what victory feels like.

The secret of landing your first customer on Periscope.tv is in shifting your mindset from claiming victory of securing that first sale to realizing that the sale is just the beginning of repeating this process over and over again.

BOOM!

YOU ARE DONE!

PERIHACKS | P.O. Box 2713 | Austin, TX 78768-2713
http://perihacks.com

Try it out and share your experience with us by leaving your thoughts on Amazon.com We would like to take a deeper look into your strategy and assist you with finding that needle in the haystack prospect on Periscope.TV. We are here to guide you through it! http://perihacks.com/bookme

PERIHACKS | P.O. Box 2713 | Austin, TX 78768-2713
http://perihacks.com

ABOUT THE AUTHOR

 **Arvin Poole** is a serial entrepreneur, digital marketing influencer, Amazon best-selling author with a passion of developing profit-generating solutions for his clients.

Arvin has founded several successful businesses, for profit and not-for profit, in the education technology, consumer products and digital information markets. He has been able to effectively build large communities, both online and offline, through his unique approach to

PERIHACKS | P.O. Box 2713 | Austin, TX 78768-2713
http://perihacks.com

delivering high quality, value-added training and education.

Arvin is also an up and coming public speaker where he is currently sharing his business experience across live-streaming platforms such as Periscope.tv, Facebook Live and MeVee. In less than 6 months, Arvin has built a strong community of over 6000 friends and followers. He leverages live streaming to deliver value-add content on topics of digital marketing, web technology and personal branding.

Arvin lives in Austin, Texas and is passionate about meeting new people, flying, traveling, teaching and most importantly, being a Dad to his two daughters, Lenea and McKenna!

PERIHACKS | P.O. Box 2713 | Austin, TX 78768-2713
http://perihacks.com